Advent Street

ADVENT STREET

Carol Ann Duffy

Illustrated by Yelena Bryksenkova

PICADOR

First published 2022 by Picador
an imprint of Pan Macmillan
The Smithson, 6 Briset Street, London EC1M 5NR
EU representative: Macmillan Publishers Ireland Ltd, 1st Floor,
The Liffey Trust Centre, 117–126 Sheriff Street Upper,
Dublin 1, DO1 YC43
Associated companies throughout the world
www.panmacmillan.com

ISBN 978-1-5290-8390-3

3 5 7 9 8 6 4 2

A CIP catalogue record for this book is available from the British Library.

Printed and bound in Spain by Graficas Estella

Visit www.picador.com to read more about all our books and to buy them.
You will also find features, author interviews and news of any author events, and
you can sign up for e-newsletters so that you're always first to hear about our new releases.

Advent Street

That was the year when
worse luck heaped on bad brought you
to Advent Street
and rented rooms over a corner shop;
a broken heart.

Dusk was the hour you ran out of words,
put on your shadow coat; anyone walking,
anyone passing-by, unnoticed.
Up one side of the street to the pub;
back down the other.

And in order to stop
your footsteps spelling a name over and over again,
you looked and fell in love
with the windows; one dark December night
after another.

In the first, a tiny tangerine bird
glowed and flared in a cage;
where an old man whistled close to the bars,
as if he were steadily blowing life
into a flame.

You observed
how the drawing of curtains grew later;
the window of that house
spotlit its silvered tree; a ballerina
poised to begin.

Or there, a garland of coloured bulbs
framed a girl at her piano;
and you stood, receiving
the phrase which started, stumbled and started…
O little town.

So, each gloaming a gift;
incremental. A boy at an upstairs window,
waving a star on a stick.
Nine Hanukkah candles,
a wicket of light.

And the Christmas trees,
juggling their fruits in the windows
or corners of rooms
and the televisions answering back
in bright cartoons.

The Madonna and infant
cheek to cheek, an icon
calmly staring down on the street.
Then the lovers, feeding each other
with spoons.

Soon came singers;
small groups, hatted and scarfed; their
songs opening doors as you passed
or paused or, once, faithlessly prayed
on your silent nights…

On your bleak, midwinter nights.
Under your coat,
your heart pined to be whole; heal,
like the sorrow sung by the carols
towards joy.

Under your coat,
who knew or cared what you were?
A dark figure, glancing up
at the moon; its attendant star,
a curious child.

The time when the windows
were playing-cards; with Jokers and Jacks,
Kings and Queens in their kitchens;
or lantern slides,
telling their nightly episodes.

Old age in its armchair.
Babies lifted from cribs, presents.
Teenagers lit by laptops – young saints
their guardians below, passing and laying
the plates onto the tables.

And only a few steps,
from where you stood,
to the door of a house *For Sale*;
but the distance – the sure turn of a key
in the lock – impossible.

Or so it seemed
in that long twelvemonth.
White lights for remembrance.
Green for beginnings.
Red for the heart.

The weather, language
lost for words. Vague rain,
smudging to mist. The clarity of frost.
Snow's same, sane utterance
lipread by streetlights.

Then loss had nothing to
add to the bell, marking the hours,
marking the hours,
from the nearby church.
You had to be there…

to see the windows of one house
fill up with neighbours, harmonising
at their wine; who waved you in
and bade you welcome.
So you did sit and eat in Advent Street.

Also by Carol Ann Duffy and available from Picador